First Questions and Answers about Farms

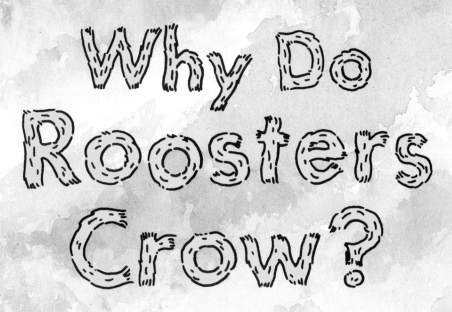

Why Do Roosters Crow?

TIME LIFE *for* Children®

ALEXANDRIA, VIRGINIA

Contents

Why do roosters crow?   4

Where do chickens come from?   6

Why are some eggs white and some brown?   8

Do goats eat tin cans?   10

What's in that building?   12

What are those big round things in the field?   14

How do dogs help out on a farm?   16

Why did that lamb follow me?   18

What are tractors for?   20

Why are we tearing up the grass?   22

How are seeds planted?   24

What's happening to the corn?   26

How is a weed different from other plants?   28

I see the tomatoes, but where are the potatoes?   30

What's so scary about a scarecrow?   32

Why is that blackberry bush being cut down?   34

Does it hurt the horse when you nail on her shoes?   36

Why do pigs like to play in the mud?   38

Who is the cat waiting for?   40

How do cows make milk?   42

What happens to the milk next?   44

Does all our food come from farms?   46

Why do roosters crow?

A rooster crows to tell other roosters, "This farm belongs to me!" The rooster is just one of many noisy animals on a farm. It crows all day long, but you notice it more at daybreak because that's when the farm is most quiet.

Where do chickens come from?

Chicks hatch from eggs that are laid by hens. If the hen mates with a rooster before she lays an egg, the egg may become fertilized. Only fertilized eggs become chicks. That's why the eggs you buy at the store could never become chicks—they have not been fertilized by a rooster.

To hatch these babies, I sat on my nest and kept the eggs warm for three weeks.

Then we poked holes in our shells...

Why are some eggs white and some brown?

White eggs come from white hens. Brown eggs come from hens that are gray or red or black. White eggs and brown eggs taste the same, and both of them are equally good for you.

Did you know?

In the South American country of Chile, there is a kind of chicken that lays greenish-blue eggs!

Do goats eat tin cans?

Goats can't chew and swallow metal, but they are always looking for a taste of something different, so sometimes they chew the paper label off a tin can. When that happens, it looks like the goat is eating the can. A goat will also nibble on cloth or wood. Most farmers give their goats a special mix of grass, hay, corn or oats, and vegetables. But even well-fed goats like to snack on twigs and leaves from fruit trees.

Did you know?

Many people can't drink cow's milk. It gives them a stomach ache. They drink goat's milk or some other special milk instead.

What's in that building?

That tall, round building is called a silo. In summer, the farmer fills the silo with corn, cornstalks, and grass stems. In winter, the farmer takes the corn and grass out of the silo and feeds it to the farm animals.

Did you know?

Not all silos look like this one. Some are tunnels or pits dug into the ground.

13

What are those big round things in the field?

Those big round things are bales of hay. Hay starts out as a crop, such as grass, clover, or alfalfa, that grows in a field. The farmer cuts the crop and lets it dry in the field. Then a special machine rolls it into tight, round shapes called bales. The bales are stored in a barn or left in the field. When winter comes, the farmer spreads the haybales on the ground to feed the farm animals.

Now where did those chicks go?

Did you know?

One big haybale can feed a cow for about two months.

15

How do dogs help out on a farm?

A dog that lives on a farm has a lot of work to do! Some farm dogs catch mice. Others chase away foxes and other animals that try to eat chickens or crops. A sheepdog is used for herding; it runs around the cattle or sheep, keeping them together in a herd as they move from the pasture to the barn.

Did you know?

Dogs trained to herd animals will herd anything: ducks, chickens, cats—even soccer balls and children!

Why did that lamb follow me?

Because it wants breakfast! The lamb's mother, called a ewe, may have had too many babies to feed. Most ewes have enough milk for only one or two lambs. When they have more than two, the farmer keeps the other lambs alive by feeding them milk from a bottle.

What are tractors for?

A tractor can do many jobs because it has big, grooved tires that help it travel over rocks and mud. The farmer hitches machines to the tractor that plow and plant the fields, mow grass, and make hay. A tractor can also spread fertilizer, dig ditches, shovel snow, pump water, and pull tree stumps out of the ground.

Did you know?

Most of the work that is now done by tractors used to be done by horses. Some small farms still use horses for plowing and planting.

Why are we tearing up the grass?

This field is being prepared for the crop that will grow in it next year. When the tractor digs up the field, it mixes the grass into the soil. This makes the soil richer. Next spring, the tractor will plow the field again, breaking up the dirt clumps and smoothing out the soil. Then the farmer can plant new seeds.

Did you know?

Land that is worked too hard provides
smaller crops. The farmer lets some
fields rest by not planting anything
on them for several months.

How are seeds planted?

A planter is one of the many machines that can be towed behind a tractor. Inside the planter is a bin full of seeds. Some planters drop the seeds from the bin in nice, neat rows. That's how corn and wheat are planted. Other planters spray the seeds all around; both hay and pasture grass are planted this way.

What's happening to the corn?

Farmers use a machine called a combine harvester to pick the corn when it is ripe. Here's how the harvester works:

First, the stalks are cut down by blades shaped like wheels. Next, the cornstalks travel into rollers that pull off the leaves; this is called shucking the corn. Other rollers shell the corn, or cut the kernels off the cobs.

Finally, the harvester unloads
the corn by spraying the
kernels through a tube into a
truck or wagon.

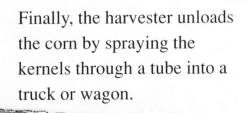

How is a weed different from other plants?

A weed is a strong, wild plant that grows so fast it crowds out the other plants in a garden. Some weeds carry insects that hurt other plants but leave the weeds alone. Chemicals can be used to kill weeds, but these chemicals are not good for people and animals to eat. The safest way to get rid of the weeds in a garden is to pull them out by the roots.

29

I see the tomatoes, but where are the potatoes?

They're growing underground! Tomatoes and potatoes both grow on vines, but the part of the potato plant that you can eat is hidden under the dirt. To harvest potatoes, the farmer has to dig them up.

Plants that give us food grow in many different ways. Apples and cherries grow on trees. Some green beans and most berries grow on bushes. Pumpkins and squashes grow on vines. Carrots, radishes, and onions all grow underground.

Did you know?

A tomato is not a vegetable—it's a fruit. Some tomatoes grow to be the size of marbles; others get to be as big as softballs.

What's so scary about a scarecrow?

A scarecrow may not look scary to you, but it frightens away birds because it looks like a person standing in the garden. Big birds such as crows and grackles have to be kept out of the garden because they can hurt it: They eat seeds, knock down cornstalks, and peck holes in the fruits and vegetables. A scarecrow keeps them away.

Did you know?
Shiny bits of foil tied to
a fence can also scare
away birds .

33

Why is that blackberry bush being cut down?

It isn't! The old stems are being cut back so strong new ones can grow. That's called pruning. Pruning is good for plants because it gives the branches more room to grow. The healthier we make these bushes, the more blackberries they will give us for jams and pies!

Does it hurt the horse when you nail on her shoes?

Not a bit! When a blacksmith nails a metal shoe onto a horse's hoof, the nails go into the hard, outer part of the hoof, which cannot feel anything. The horseshoes keep this outer part from wearing away. That's important, because the outer part of the hoof protects a softer part inside.

Why do pigs like to play in the mud?

Because it keeps them cool! People cool off by sweating, but pigs don't sweat. They need another way to beat the heat, so they lie down in water or in nice, cool mud. The mud also keeps insects from biting or stinging the pigs.

Who is the cat waiting for?

That big barn cat is probably waiting to catch a mouse or a rat. Mice and rats are a big problem on many farms because they eat up the grain that the farmer has been saving for the cows and sheep. The mice and rats make their nests in hay stored in the barn. Hunting down these pesky critters is the barn cat's main job.

How do cows make milk?

A cow's body makes milk from the grass, hay, and grain that she eats every day. The cow begins to make milk when she has a baby, called a calf. She makes more milk than her calf needs, so the farmer takes the extra.

Did you know?

Cows need to be milked at least twice a day. On big farms with lots of cows, milking machines do the job.

What happens to the milk next?

The farm family keeps some of the milk for drinking. It turns the rest of the milk into all kinds of good food, from butter and cheese to yogurt, cream cheese, and ice cream.

Does all our food come from farms?

Just about everything we eat began on a farm. The cereal you have for breakfast started out as grain in a field. The fruit in your lunch grew on trees in an orchard. And the vegetables on your dinner plate were picked from a garden patch, large or small. In one year, an acre of land on a small farm can produce more than 10 truckloads of food.

47

TIME-LIFE for CHILDREN®

Managing Editor: Patricia Daniels
Editorial Directors: Jean Burke Crawford, Allan Fallow,
       Sara Mark
Senior Art Director: Susan K. White
Publishing Associate: Marike van der Veen
Administrative Assistant: Mary M. Saxton
Production Manager: Marlene Zack
Senior Copyeditor: Colette Stockum
Quality Assurance Manager: Miriam P. Newton
Library: Louise D. Forstall, Anne Heising

Special Contributor: Barbara Klein
Researcher: Jocelyn Lindsay
Writer: Jacqueline A. Ball

Designed by: David Bennett Books

Series design: David Bennett
Book design: David Bennett
Art direction: David Bennett
Illustrated by: Peter Kavanagh and Jim Kavanagh
Additional cover
 illustrations by: Nick Baxter

First printing. Printed in U.S.A.
Published simultaneously in Canada.

Time Life Inc. is a wholly owned subsidiary of THE TIME INC. BOOK COMPANY.

TIME-LIFE is a trademark of Time Warner Inc. U.S.A.
For subscription information, call 1-800-621-7026.

Library of Congress Cataloging-in-Publication Data

Why do roosters crow? : first questions and answers about the farm. p. cm.– (Time-Life library of first questions and answers)
ISBN 0-7835-0899-9 (hardcover)
1. Farms–Miscellanea–Juvenile literature. 2. Agriculture–Miscellanea–Juvenile literature. 3. Farm life–Miscellanea–Juvenile literature. 4. Domestic animals–Miscellanea–Juvenile literature. [1. Farms–Miscellanea. 2. Agriculture–Miscellanea. 3. Farm
life–Miscellanea. 4. Domestic animals–Miscellanea. 5. Questions and answers.] I.Time-Life for Children (Firm) II. Title: First
questions and answers about the farm. III. Series: Library of first questions and answers.
S519.W48 1995   93-33315

630—dc20   CIP
                            AC

Consultants

Dr. Lewis P. Lipsitt, an internationally recognized specialist on childhood
   development, was the 1990 recipient of the Nicholas Hobbs Award for science in the
   service of children. He has served as the science director for the American
   Psychological Association and is a professor of psychology and medical science at
   Brown University, where he directed the Child Study Center from 1968 to 1993.

Thomas D. Mullin directs the Beaver Brook Association in Hollis, New Hampshire, where
   he coordinates workshops and seminars designed to promote appreciation for wildlife
   and the environment.

Dr. Judith A. Schickedanz, an authority on the education of preschool children, is an associate professor of early childhood education at the Boston University School of
   Education, where she also directs the Early Childhood Learning Laboratory. Her published work includes *More Than the ABCs: Early Stages of Reading and Writing* as well
   as several textbooks and many scholarly papers.